THE
VEGETABLE
GARDENER'S
JOURNAL

Text by
Oliver E. Allen
◆
Illustrations by
Mary Rankin

THE
VEGETABLE
GARDENER'S
JOURNAL

STEWART
TABORI
& CHANG

PUBLISHERS, NEW YORK

Designed by Nai Y. Chang

Text copyright © 1985 by Oliver E. Allen

Illustrations copyright © 1985 by Mary Rankin

ISBN: 0-941434-63-X

Published in 1985 by
Stewart, Tabori & Chang, Inc., New York.

Distributed by Workman Publishing,
1 West 39 Street, New York, New York 10018.

Printed and bound in Japan.

Cicorium intybus

CONTENTS

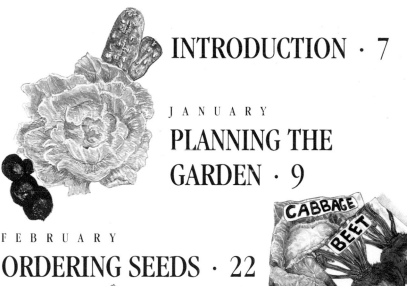

INTRODUCTION

This book is a journal of your personal gardening experience. It is also a planning guide and a month-by-month record that you yourself will write, often just after coming in from the garden. Every knowledgeable vegetable grower knows the value of keeping detailed notes and records. Because such things as planting dates, types of fertilizers used, ways of protecting against harmful insects, and the combined influence of temperature and rainfall can significantly affect the size and quality of your yields, and because there are so many kinds and varieties of vegetables to choose from, it is vital to keep track of exactly when and how you have taken each step in the complex process. Only that way will you be able to better your garden's performance from year to year and make vegetable growing as rewarding and pleasurable as you know it can be.

The book is organized on a month-to-month basis. Each month's chapter leads off with a short essay summing up the main concerns that you will likely be focusing on during that time, together with some general advice on what to do. The choice of topics for each month is based on gardening conditions likely to be found in the moderate climate zones stretching roughly across the middle of the U.S.—where the last frost in the springtime will occur between mid-April and mid-May, and the first autumn frost between mid-September and the end of October. Gardeners living outside those zones, with temperatures either generally colder or somewhat warmer, should be able to adjust for local conditions without difficulty.

The remainder of each chapter takes the form of a journal that suggests tasks for that month and provides space for listing your own accomplishments and observations. There are also blank pages at the end of the book for records of planting, of harvest, and so on. There is no reason to feel that every blank should be filled in; use your own judgment. Feel free, also, to enter any random personal observations and concerns in the spaces provided at the end of each chapter.

Although the book is based on the calendar year, many gardeners will be acquiring it midway in the season. That should pose no problem. Scan the book to see how it works, and then just begin using it at the appropriate moment or go back and fill in what information you remember. Record-keeping can start any time. And so can successful vegetable gardening.

Daucus carota

PLANNING THE GARDEN

With winter holding sway, the first weeks of the new year offer a chance to indulge in the pleasures of planning the coming season's vegetable garden. As the seed catalogues begin arriving, experienced gardeners ponder ways to improve on last year's output, while newcomers are enticed by gloriously imagined bounties. The challenge is to keep the garden patch producing throughout the season, yielding a succession of succulent harvests. It is a quest all the more intriguing as every garden is unique. There is no one way to raise vegetables.

All vegetables can be classified according to their reaction to cold or warm temperatures. And veteran practitioners know that the key to continuous productivity lies in orchestrating the response of the different types of vegetables: planting in early spring the crops that flourish at that time, replacing them in early summer with ones that thrive during warmer days, and again planting in mid- or late summer for a fall crop. Keeping in mind the recommended planting dates and the number of days to maturity of each crop (a figure generally given in the seed catalogues), the wily grower can set up a rough schedule for a rewarding year.

Two other things help govern the choice of crops and where they are grown. One is light (see box on page 12); another is yield. Although yields per square foot can vary widely, seed packets are frequently based on planting a 15-foot row; for planning purposes you can estimate that a conventional 15-foot row can supply a family of three handily (check also the yield chart on page 86). But alternative methods of planting can affect yield. Looseleaf lettuce, parsley, peas, carrots, parsnips, beets, and radishes can be planted in wide rows— up to 15 inches across—or in blocks, with the seed scattered virtually at random and with yields multiplying. Such plants as pole beans or cucumbers can be grown on vertical supports; obviously, this will increase your yield per square foot. Raised beds, in which the soil is mounded up (and sometimes enclosed by boards or bricks), provide for better drainage; this allows soil to warm faster, often increasing the yield. And many gardeners practice what is called interplanting, growing two crops like radishes and beets together; the radishes come up and are harvested by the time the beets take over. To be sure, you may decide to overproduce deliberately so as to allow for preserving or even giving away your surpluses (see September for information on canning and the like).

In plotting the year's schedule, be sure to allow for succession: when one crop is in, its space can be used to grow another (see June for details). But, unless you can find someone to mind your garden while you are away, avoid raising crops that will produce their fruits just as you are departing for vacation.

Whatever the planting scheme you decide on, remember to rotate crops. Switching vegetables around from year to year helps prevent disease and also equalizes the demand on the soil, thus forestalling deficiencies. But note that some crops may do poorly when succeeding others: beans, for example, may not do well planted where onions have just grown, nor may tomatoes or potatoes successfully follow any of the brassicas (cabbages, broccoli, and cauliflower among others).

Lastly, two major rules govern placement. Vegetables that grow tall, whether by themselves (corn) or on supports (tomatoes), should be placed at the side of the garden, say in the northeast corner, where they will not shade smaller plants. And perennials like asparagus and rhubarb should go into a section by themselves so that the spading and tilling required annually will not disturb them.

CHECKLIST FOR JANUARY

☐ Choose crops to grow this year

☐ Draw up a month-by-month planting schedule

☐ Sketch the proposed garden

TEMPERATURE NEEDS

Except for perennials, which can be planted at any time, all vegetables should go into the ground at a time appropriate to their temperature requirements, as shown below. *Hardy* crops can be planted four to six weeks before the last likely frost date in your area; *half-hardy* ones can go into the ground a couple of weeks before that date. *Tender* vegetables should be planted only after the average frost date has passed, while *very tender* ones must wait a week or two more, until all danger of frost is gone. To find your last-frost date, consult your local County Agent and check with neighbors who are familiar with growing conditions in your immediate area. In milder sections of the U.S., many of the hardy crops are planted in late autumn to overwinter in the ground. Vegetables marked with an * are best for fall; planted in midsummer, they will survive the first autumn frost and produce during October and November. Those marked # cannot stand summer heat.

COOL-SEASON CROPS		WARM-SEASON CROPS	
HARDY	HALF-HARDY	TENDER	VERY TENDER
Broccoli	Beets	Cowpeas	Cucumbers
*Brussels	Carrots	New Zealand	Eggplant
sprouts	*#Cauliflower	spinach	Lima beans
Cabbage	Celery	Pole beans	Muskmelon
Collards	Chinese	Snap beans	Okra
Garlic	cabbage	Soybeans	Peppers
*Kale	Endive	Sweet corn	Pumpkins
Kohlrabi	Mustard		Squash
Leeks	Parsnips		Sweet potatoes
#Lettuce	Potatoes		Tomatoes
Onions	Rutabaga		Watermelon
#Peas	Salsify		
Radishes	Swiss chard		
#Spinach			
#Turnips			

SOURCE: adapted from United States Department of Agriculture chart, with additional information from W. B. Johnson.

GROWING SPANS

Group 1 crops are perennials, which occupy their space in the garden for a year or more. *Group 2* crops may be planted early on and will occupy the ground only for the first part of the season. *Group 3* crops occupy the ground for most of the season. *Group 4* crops may be planted in midsummer or later and harvested in the fall.

GROUP 1	GROUP 2	GROUP 3	GROUP 4
Artichokes	Early beets	Brussels sprouts	Beets
Asparagus	Early cabbage	Bush and pole	Bush beans
Chives	Early spinach	beans	Broccoli
Horseradish	Lettuce	Carrots	Cauliflower
Rhubarb	Mustard	Celery	Chinese cabbage
	Onion sets	Eggplant	Collards
	Peas	Lima beans	Endive
	Radishes	Muskmelon	Kale
	Turnips	Okra	Kohlrabi
		Peppers	Lettuce
		Pumpkins	Radishes
		Sweet corn	Spinach
		Swiss chard	Turnips
		Tomatoes	
		Watermelon	

Note: Some cool-season crops, notably spinach and lettuce, are suitable for planting either for very early or for late harvest. However, they do not stand heat well; if you are considering these for fall harvest, plant as late in the season as possible. Cabbages, depending on their variety, may be either a spring crop, a summer crop, or a fall crop. Squash may be either an early summer variety or a fall-harvest variety. Cucumbers occupy the ground from midspring until late summer, as do potatoes.

SOURCE: adapted from Raymond, *Down-to-Earth Vegetable Gardening Know-How*; data from the Cooperative Extension Service of the University of West Virginia.

SUNLIGHT NEEDED

MINIMUM DAILY HOURS OF SUNLIGHT	TYPE OF VEGETABLE
4	Leafy greens
6	Root crops
8	Fruit formers

DAYS TO MATURITY

Seed packets, and most seed catalogues, usually list the number of days
needed between planting and the time when a vegetable begins to
produce. Bear in mind that this refers to the total time spent in a
growing environment: if you start a crop indoors, its days-to-maturity
span begins at that moment—not when you transplant it outdoors later.

COMPANION PLANTING

*In placing crops, you may want to heed what is called companion
planting, the notion that some crops seem to do better if planted near
certain others. Chives, parsley, and garlic, for example, may help prevent
insects from attacking other crops; onions, however, should be kept away
from beans. Many herbs are reputed to possess odors that repel insects
(basil may help protect tomatoes), and marigolds traditionally protect
against nematodes. Note, however, that such theories are unproven, and
many horticulturists dispute them.*

(See also companion planting note for July, page 72.)

CROPS TO GROW

CROP	PLANTING DATE	ESTIMATED HARVEST DATE

CROPS TO GROW

CROP	PLANTING DATE	ESTIMATED HARVEST DATE

MONTH-BY-MONTH PLANTING SCHEDULE

January	
February	
March	
April	
May	
June	

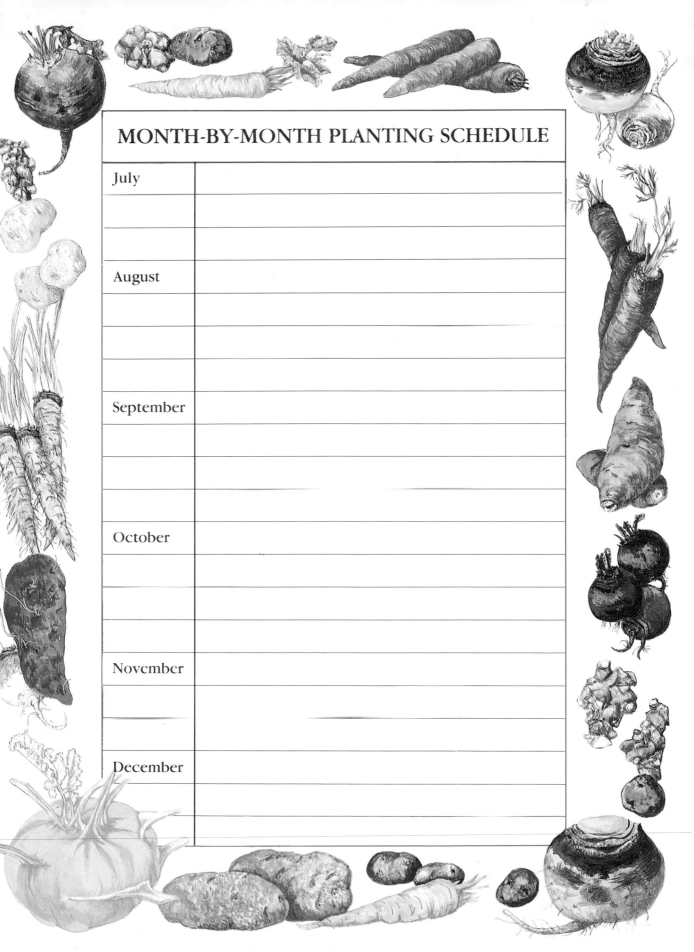

MONTH-BY-MONTH PLANTING SCHEDULE

July	
August	
September	
October	
November	
December	

SKETCH OF GARDEN

Space rows according to the size of the mature plant, but allow extra room if you use a mechanical tiller or cultivator. Consider working in pencil, so adjustments can be easily made. You may also want to use different colors to indicate plants in different categories (perennials, early spring crops, etc.) so as to distinguish those that occupy the same space in succession. You might want to list proposed planting dates for each crop.

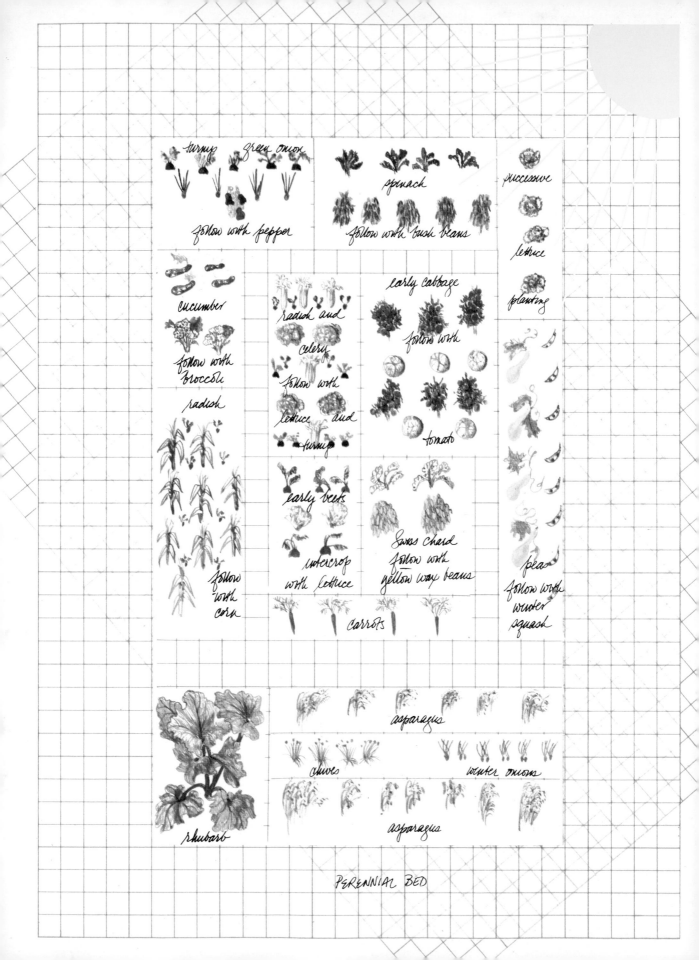

turnip green onion

follow with pepper

spinach

follow with bush beans

successive

lettuce

planting

cucumber

follow with broccoli

radish

radish and

celery

follow with

lettuce and

turnip

early cabbage

follow with

tomato

peas

follow with winter squash

early beets

intercrop with lettuce

Swiss chard follow with yellow wax beans

carrots

rhubarb

asparagus

chives   winter onions

asparagus

PERENNIAL BED

JANUARY NOTES

Name, address, and phone of County Agent ❧ Crops to try this year ❧ Crops most successful last year ❧ Special information about a plant ❧ Last frost (projected) ❧ First frost (projected)

It is a good thing for a gardener to keep a diary. . . . The diary would take note of everything that happened in the garden. The sowing of seeds would be recorded; also when the seedlings first appear; when they are thinned out, and when they blossom: in fact, everything to do with the life of the plants.

—E.V. Lucas and E. Lucas

ORDERING SEEDS

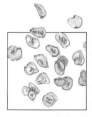

For most gardeners, February is seed-buying time. Indeed, some growers will have already gotten a jump on the season by ordering in January. Although planting outdoors may not get under way for a month or two, you can stretch the growing season by starting seeds indoors well in advance of the last frost date. Make sure you have enough window sill space or some other well-lit facility for your seed flats. (See March for detailed information.)

A major question is how many of your crops you expect actually to grow from seed. Later in the spring, neighborhood garden centers sell vegetable plants grown under controlled conditions in greenhouses, and

it is possible to set out an entire garden with them. They are familiarly known as transplants. Some vegetables, to be sure, must almost necessarily be started indoors to do well in the average garden; among them are tomatoes, the so-called cole crops (cabbages, broccoli, cauliflower, Brussels sprouts, collards, kale, and kohlrabi), peppers, eggplant, cucumbers, and squash. Many gardeners habitually buy these as transplants, or start them from seed in their own homes; and they plant everything else outdoors from seed. Buying an entire vegetable patch in transplant form may make sense if your season is short or you lack the time to start crops indoors. It is, however, an expensive way to garden. Seeds are cheap.

Seeds can be bought either by mail or off the rack at a garden center or supermarket. Racks offer instant availability, but some sellers allow packets to remain on sale too long; check the date on the packet to make sure the seed is viable. Mail-order concerns generally offer a far wider selection than local stores and are likelier to have new strains. Consulting several catalogues can give you a large choice of seeds to buy.

From any established firm, virtually every packet will be reliable and capable of producing a satisfactory harvest. To choose among varieties, you can check with friends and neighbors, or buy varieties that firms have specifically developed and promoted over the years, or go with the "All-American Winners." These are recently introduced strains that have been awarded this designation on the basis of impartial nationwide testing, and some gardeners happily buy nothing else. You may also want to check your County Agent or local agricultural college for recommendations.

Seeds for hybrid vegetables are offered in most catalogues. They are more expensive than the open-pollinated types (those that will produce conventional strains), but they have superior qualities such as copious yields, high disease resistance, or the ability to bear early. Make sure the added qualities—they are usually specified in the seed catalogue or on the packet—are worth the extra expense.

CHECKLIST FOR FEBRUARY

☐ Decide on seeds vs. transplants

☐ Order seeds

☐ Check supplies

☐ Start some seeds indoors

☐ Keep seed flats moist

TESTING FOR VIABILITY

Seeds left over from last year may be used this year if they can be judged viable. To test, place a dozen or so seeds on a moistened paper towel, enclose the towel in a plastic bag, and seal it. Keep the bag in a warm spot for ten days (only about a week in the case of lettuce), and inspect it every few days. If, at the end of the period, at least half the seeds have germinated, the batch can be considered viable. If not, discard them and buy new seed.

Note: If you have collected seeds from plants grown last year, they should perform much as if newly purchased. But don't save seeds from hybrids, as they are unlikely to reproduce their parents exactly.

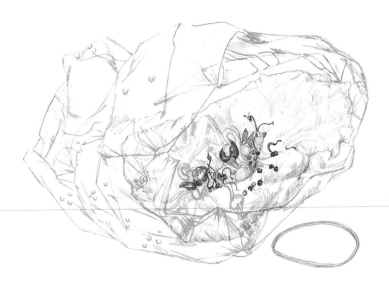

SOME CATALOGUE TERMS

"Disease resistant" means that a certain strain is extremely unlikely to succumb to particular diseases, although no plant can be guaranteed totally immune. "Disease tolerant," on the other hand, designates a strain that may acquire certain ailments but probably will survive if properly treated. "Untreated seed" designates seed that has not been treated with a fungicide to forestall rotting and disease. Many seeds are so treated automatically, but seed companies can often send you untreated seed if you so request.

SEED INNOVATIONS

Seed tape, in which seeds are bound at appropriate intervals into a biodegradable strip, makes for convenience in planting: you need only place the tape in a furrow and cover it. But under certain circumstances the tape can buckle, pushing some seeds out of the ground. Seed pellets are more practical: they provide a bulky but dissolvable covering for tiny seeds (such as those for carrots and lettuce) that are hard to handle. Gardeners weary of having seeds disappear between their fingers welcome the pellets. But the ground in which seed pellets are planted must be kept moist enough for the covering to dissolve—if it does not dissolve, the seed will not germinate. This can be a problem especially with lettuce seeds, which some companies recommend planting on top of the soil; if the moisture is too plentiful the seeds may float away.

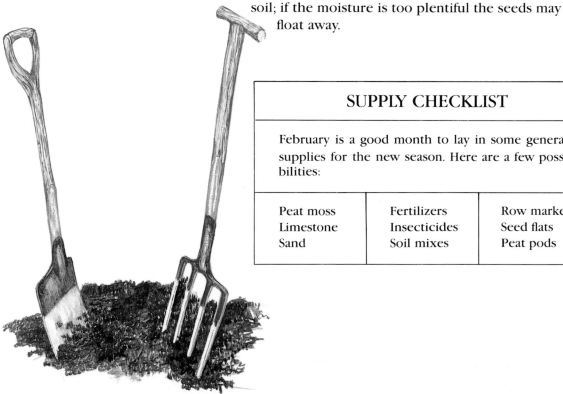

SUPPLY CHECKLIST

February is a good month to lay in some general supplies for the new season. Here are a few possibilities:

Peat moss	Fertilizers	Row markers
Limestone	Insecticides	Seed flats
Sand	Soil mixes	Peat pods

MAIL-ORDER SEED COMPANIES

All the firms listed below are reliable, and their catalogues are all free.

Agrigenetics Seed Co.
P.O. Box 1438
Hollister, CA 95023

Agway Inc.
Box 4741
Syracuse, NY 13221

Burgess Seed & Plant Co.
905 Four Seasons Road
Bloomington, IL 61701

Burrell Seed Co.
P.O. Box 150
Rocky Ford, CO 81067

DeGiorgi Co.
P.O. Box 413
Council Bluffs, IA 51501

Earl May Seed & Nursery Co.
Shenandoah, IA 51603

Farmer Seed & Nursery Co.
P.O. Box 129
Faribault, MI 55021

George W. Park Seed Company
Greenwood, SC 29647

Gurney Seed & Nursery Co.
Yankton, SD 57079

Harris Moran Seed Co.
3670 Buffalo Road
Rochester, NY 14624

H.G. Hastings Co.
Box 4274
Atlanta, GA 30302

Johnny's Selected Seeds
Albion, ME 04910

J.W. Jung Seed Co.
Randolph, WI 53956

Kilgore Seed Co., Inc.
1400 1 Street
Sanford, FL 32771

L. L. Olds Seed Co.
P.O. Box 7790
Madison, WI 53707

Stokes Seeds Inc.
28 Water Street
Sradonia, NY 14063
(also, P.O. Box 10
St. Catherines
Ontario L2R 6R6
Canada)

Thompson & Morgan
P.O. Box 1308
Jackson, NJ 08527

W. Atlee Burpee Co.
300 Park Avenue
Warminster, PA 18974

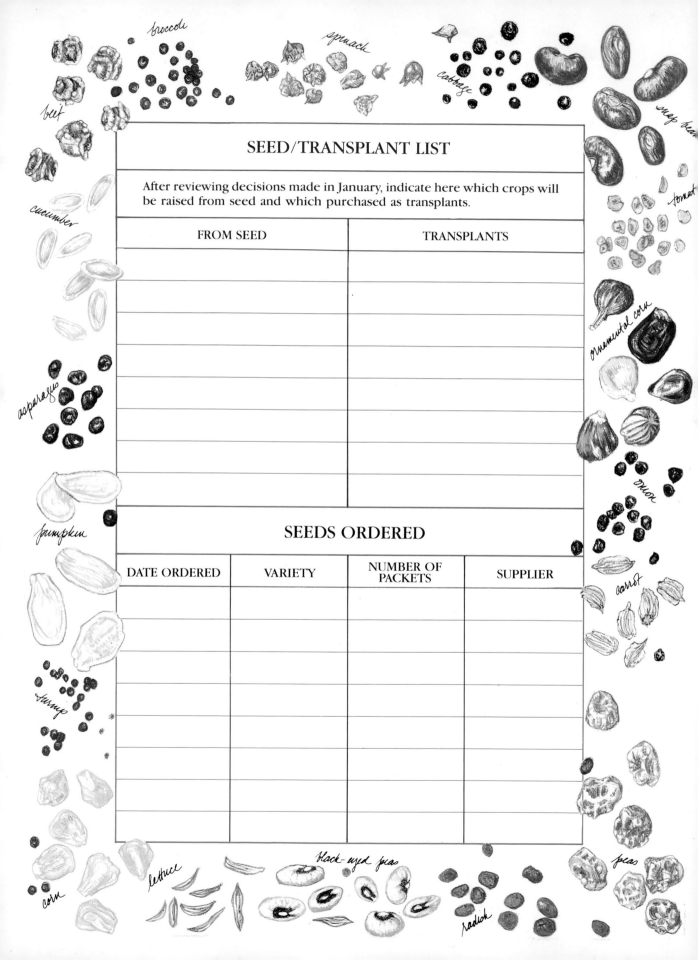

SEED/TRANSPLANT LIST

After reviewing decisions made in January, indicate here which crops will be raised from seed and which purchased as transplants.

FROM SEED	TRANSPLANTS

SEEDS ORDERED

DATE ORDERED	VARIETY	NUMBER OF PACKETS	SUPPLIER

SEEDS STARTED INDOORS THIS MONTH

DATE SOWN	CROP	PLANTING MIX	DATE SPROUTS REPOTTED

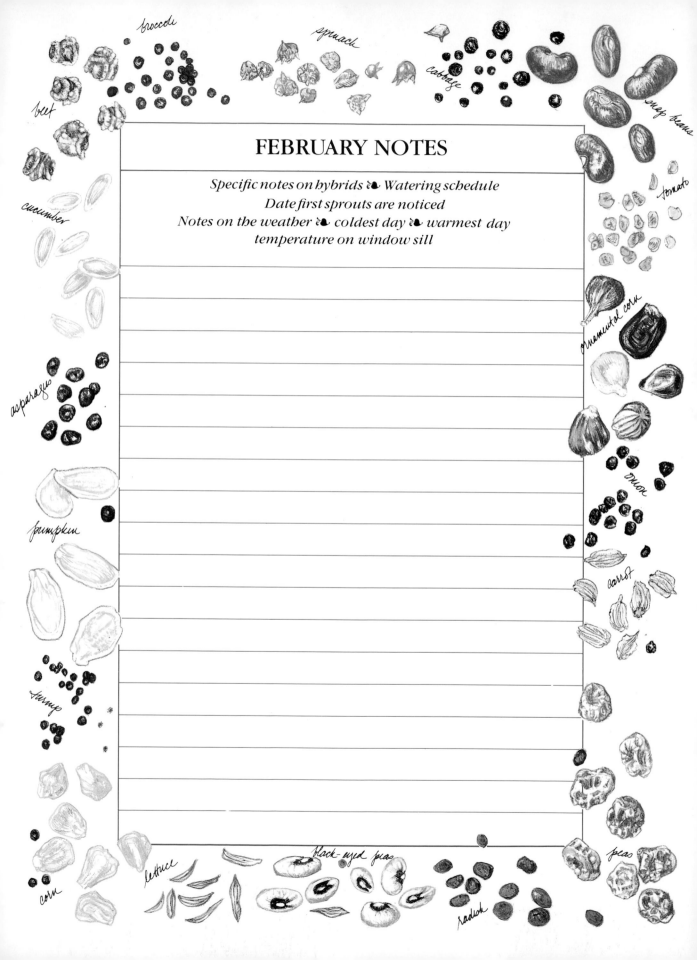

FEBRUARY NOTES

Specific notes on hybrids ❧ Watering schedule
Date first sprouts are noticed
Notes on the weather ❧ coldest day ❧ warmest day
temperature on window sill

FEBRUARY NOTES

All work is as seed sown; it grows and spreads, and sows itself anew.

—THOMAS CARLYLE

FERTILIZERS

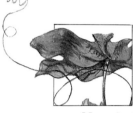

A blustery month of change and transition in which the weather is typically unsettled, March beckons the gardener outdoors. By the end of the month, at least in the middle temperature zones across the U.S., the soil can be worked and a number of crops can be set into the ground.

Now is the time to make sure the garden soil is fully prepared to receive and nurture crops. Even if you have carried out a thoroughgoing renovation program the previous autumn (following the plan outlined in November), you will want to inspect the soil at this time for both friability and chemical balance. Remember the familiar clump test. Pick up a handful of soil and squeeze it into a clump: it should hold together by itself but break apart when knocked or dropped. If it doesn't hold together, it is too light, dry, or sandy; but if it stays clumped even when dropped, it is too wet, or has too high a clay content, or both. If too light, add organic matter (peat moss or compost); if too heavy, lighten with peat moss or sand. Check also on the soil's acidity level and nutrient content, either using your own testing kit (available at garden centers) or sending a sample to the local County Agent. After learning the test results, make any necessary corrections as indicated by the test kit instructions or the Agent's report.

Adjusting for content or consistency can be combined with the first tilling. No matter how often the soil has been turned over in the past, it must be thoroughly tilled now to a depth of 8 to 12 inches before planting—unless you use a permanent mulch (see May). Add the first application of fertilizer before tilling, so that the proper nutrients will be well mixed in with the soil.

While awaiting warmer weather, foresighted gardeners will continue starting seeds indoors—not only beets, lettuce, and onions (which may have been started in February) but cabbage, broccoli, and cauliflower, and perhaps tomatoes toward the end of the month. Seedlings that have reached transplanting size can be hardened off by being set outdoors in their flats for a spell each day for ten days, or by being transferred to a cold frame if you have one. Such acclimating is necessary to ensure the young plants' readiness to survive in the still-cool garden.

Depending on the frost date in your area, some crops (peas, spinach, radishes) may be seeded directly into the ground before the month is out, and you can keep track of this planting in the blanks on pages 108–111. (For planting guidelines, see April.) Be doubly sure from the outset to institute adequate controls against pests and diseases—such sly marauders as slugs and cutworms will soon enough be a problem. (For a discussion of pests and diseases and their remedies, see July.) After all, a measure of vigilance is a small price to pay for what should be great rewards as the season goes on.

Pisum sativum

CHECKLIST FOR MARCH

☐   Test soil for consistency and content

☐   Begin tilling soil

☐   Start seeds indoors

☐   Water seeds

☐   Harden off seedlings

☐   Plant some crops outdoors

☐   Keep seed flats moist

☐   Begin pest and disease management

ACIDITY LEVELS

Most vegetables prefer a soil that is slightly on the acid side. As the neutral point on the pH scale (by which alkalinity and acidity are measured) is 7.0 on a scale of 0 to 14, the figure to aim for is somewhere between 6.0 and 6.8. If your soil's reading is higher than that, increase its acidity by adding ground agricultural sulfur; if it is lower and thus too acid, add ground agricultural limestone.

Testing can be done either the previous fall or in early March (to allow time for test results to come back if you have sent samples to your County Agent or other testing service).

ACIDITY TEST

DATE SAMPLE SENT OR TEST TAKEN		
RESULTS		
ADJUSTMENTS RECOMMENDED		
ACTION TAKEN		

FERTILIZING AND SIDE DRESSING

To navigate through the somewhat confusing world of fertilizers, it may make sense to follow the advice of your County Agent or of a knowledgeable authority at an established garden center. Remember that leafy crops have a particular need for nitrogen, while root crops require more phosphorus. Slow-release fertilizers, which take effect over a period of time, are more efficient than the quick-release type, but sometimes the quick release is needed to give one crop a boost. Natural fertilizers (bone meal, animal manures, seaweed, compost) and chemical ones (usually sold in granular form) have similar nutritional effects on plants; but natural ones, though they supply nutrients more slowly, can help build up the soil and thus improve the planting environment. Many practiced gardeners use a combination of both. (Remember that horse manure must be well rotted lest it burn the plant roots.)

Experts recommend fertilizing in two stages. At tilling time add an all-purpose fertilizer (or whatever has been advised), mixing it fully into the soil. Then when plants later begin to blossom or fruit, apply what is known as a side-dressing, scattering an appropriate mix on both sides of the planting row some 6 or 8 inches out, to reach the feeder roots. Repeat the side-dressing as needed.

INDOOR STARTING

Almost any kind of shallow container—cut-down milk carton, paper cup, seed flat, plastic pot—will serve to get seeds started. For a growing medium, use a commercial soilless mix or make your own using equal parts of vermiculite and peat moss. Scatter the seeds over the top of the mix and cover lightly with just a fraction of an inch of fine soil or washed sand. Keep the container moist and out of direct sun until sprouts appear; maintain moisture level either by bottom-watering (setting the container in a dish of water until the soil on top feels damp) or by enclosing the container in a plastic bag. When sprouts appear, move the container to full sunlight (or set it under plant lights) and make sure the soil does not dry out. After sprouts have grown their first true leaves, select the strongest and move them to roomier containers with richer soil.

SEEDS STARTED INDOORS THIS MONTH

DATE SOWN	CROP	PLANTING MIX	DATE SPROUTS REPOTTED

PROTECTION

Many crops can be assured a reasonably healthy life if protected right from planting time. If pea seeds or other seeds susceptible to fungus have not been treated with a fungicide, it is a good idea to apply one. Similarly, root crops will need protection against root maggots. For materials to use, check with your County Agent, and be sure to follow directions on product labels. (See July for additional information.)

PEST AND DISEASE CONTROL

DATE	SYMPTOM	CONTROL	WHERE AND HOW APPLIED	RESULTS

MARCH NOTES

Tilling ❧ Fertilizing
Date sprouts noticed outdoors ❧ Transplants hardened off
Weather this month ❧ rainfall ❧ temperature ❧ humidity

MARCH NOTES

To own a bit of ground, to scratch it with a hoe, to plant seeds, and watch the renewal of life—this is the commonest delight of the race, the most satisfactory thing a man can do.

—CHARLES DUDLEY WARNER

Asparagus officinalis

APRIL

PLANTING

 Across most of the U.S., April is the major planting month. Showers soften the earth, warm days give a hint of summer to come, and frosts become rare. Many crops can now be seeded directly into the ground, while others may be ready for transplanting from their indoor starting flats or containers into the garden outside. A final batch can be started indoors for transplanting outdoors next month. For those gardeners who elect to start their garden largely using transplants purchased from a garden center, April is surely a big buying month.

Cautious growers, while relying for general purposes on the when-to-plant charts (see pages 11–12), will want to keep an eye on the weather and, if necessary, check with the local County Agent to be absolutely sure. It's safer to plant later rather than sooner—seeds need warmth to germinate; and if the soil is too cool and wet, some seeds may rot.

When you do plant, be sure to allow ample space between rows. (Doublecheck the plan you drew up in January.) Seed packets specify the room needed, but you may want to increase the spacing to allow for a cultivator's wheels to pass easily. Packets also specify the distance to allow between seeds within a furrow, basing the figure on the size of the fully grown plant. If you are planting in hills, you may want to sow four to six seeds at each point as insurance against failure to germinate. When and if all have sprouted you can thin to the strongest of the group.

Remember that seedlings of vegetables started indoors, whether in your own home or in a commercial grower's greenhouse, must be hardened off before being trans planted into the garden—unless all cool weather is safely past. When buying transplants, make sure they have already been hardened off.

To transfer seedlings into the garden, pick an overcast day or wait until late afternoon to avoid exposing the young plants to the sun's hot rays. Soak the containers just before removing the plants, and be sure to keep as much soil around the roots as possible during the transfer. Set the plant into the ground slightly deeper than it was in the flat, and water it well. If nights are likely to be cold during the next few weeks, protect against frost by covering the young plants with plastic or paper caps when the thermometer shows signs of plummeting. Be sure to remove the protection during the day or when the weather turns warmer.

A word of caution: purchase transplants only when you are ready to plant. Surely, the urge to get going is hard to curb and should not be discouraged, but transplants bought in a rush of enthusiasm and then left for a couple of weeks before being set into the ground may get too large, dry out, or otherwise deteriorate. Ideally the new acquisitions should go into the ground the same day.

CHECKLIST FOR APRIL

☐ Review the plan for your garden

☐ Till any areas not already tilled

☐ Harden off transplants

☐ Plant seeds, or set transplants into ground

☐ Continue pest management

☐ Start seeds indoors

☐ Keep seeds moist

☐ Start weeding

☐ Protect young plants from frost

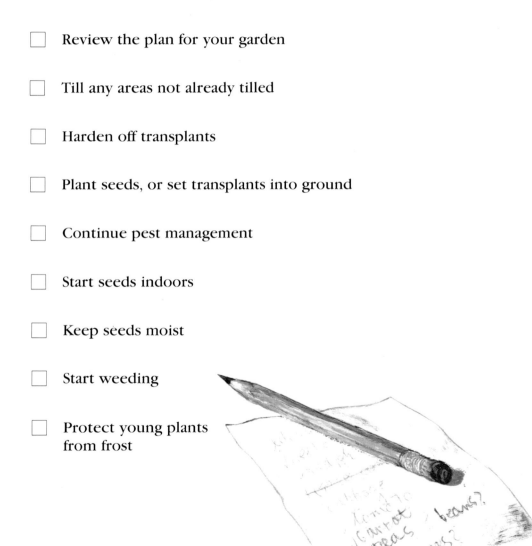

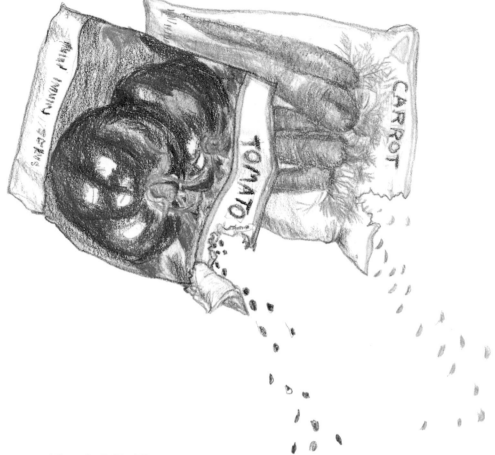

PLANTING DEPTH

The depth at which seeds should be planted varies between crops. An old rule of thumb directs that seeds be planted at a depth twice their diameter, but seed packets may direct otherwise. At this time of year it is vital to plant no deeper than specified. Later on, when the soil has become hot and dry, a second sowing of the same crop can be set deeper to prevent the seed from drying out. Cover seeds with light soil and firm the soil with your foot or with the back of a rake or hoe. Water gently and keep the soil moist until sprouts appear. When planting, you may want to set a wide board between the rows to stand on so as to avoid compacting the soil; the ground must be kept loose as it will later play host to the plant's spreading roots.

SAVING SEEDS

It is a good idea to save any leftover seeds once you have planted a crop. The extras can be used to fill in bare spots where the first sowing has failed to germinate or to start a second planting a few weeks later that will extend the harvest. Store the seeds in a covered glass jar in the refrigerator.

SOME PLANTING SIGNS

Spring weather can be contrary, so some gardeners rely on changes in the world of nature to decide when to plant. Some of these signs have become legend. In The Country Journal Book of Vegetable Gardening, *Nancy Bubel has set down a number of them.*

> *When snowdrops bloom, plant peas, lettuce, and onion sets.*
>
> *Wait until crocuses are up to plant carrots, spinach, lettuce, and radishes.*
>
> *If tulips are in bloom, it's safe to plant beets.*
>
> *You may plant Swiss chard when maple blossoms are out.*
>
> *When daffodils are in bloom, you can plant parsnips, salsify, and Hamburg-rooted parsley.*
>
> *As soon as apple trees blossom, you may plant bush beans and sweet corn.*
>
> *As the apple blossom petals fall, it's safe to plant pole beans, cucumbers, eggplant, and peppers.*
>
> *When oak leaves are the size of a mouse's ear, it's safe to plant soybeans.*
>
> *When oak leaves are the size of a squirrel's ear, it's time to plant corn.*
>
> *The time to plant lima beans and okra is when peonies are in bloom.*

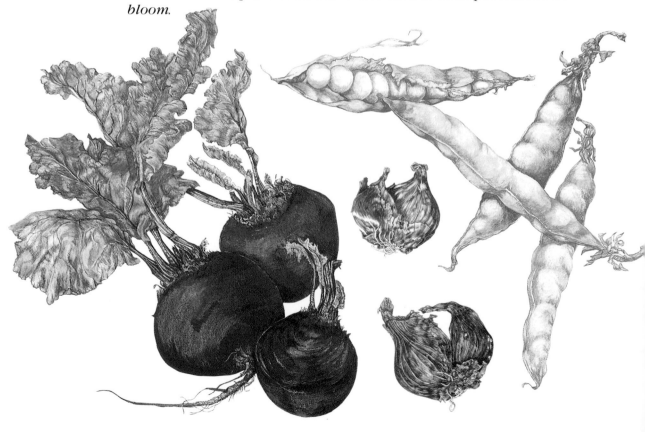

PEST ADVISORY

A number of pests make their presence especially known in April. Aphids, which attack beans and other vegetables, can be controlled by dousing the plants with a water spray. Extra handfuls of limestone applied to newly planted rows of broccoli can usually inhibit clubroot, while the cutworm that can afflict all cabbage-type crops can be repelled by installing a paper collar around each young seedling in the garden—many growers use an inverted paper cup, with the bottom removed, to protect each plant. (For more information on pests, see July.)

PEST AND DISEASE CONTROL

DATE	SYMPTOM	CONTROL	WHERE AND HOW APPLIED	RESULTS

TRANSPLANT SOLUTION

To get transplants off to a strong start in the garden on cool days, some experts recommend giving them a dose of water-soluble fertilizer (at the rate shown on the label) just when they are set into the ground. Formulas differ, but because good root growth is essential at the outset, you may want to administer a fertilizer strong in phosphorus (say 10-50-10 or 15-30-15). Pour a cupful of the solution around the roots as you set the plant in. In warm weather, plain water is adequate if fertilizer was previously tilled into the soil.

PLANTING CORN

Corn is unlike most other vegetables in that it is wind-pollinated: the pollen must be blown from the male tassels onto the female silk. If corn is planted in a single row, the resulting cobs may be less than fully developed. The solution is to plant three or four short rows about 2 feet apart instead of a single row.

SEEDS STARTED INDOORS

DATE SOWN	DROP	PLANTING MIX	DATE SPROUTS REPOTTED

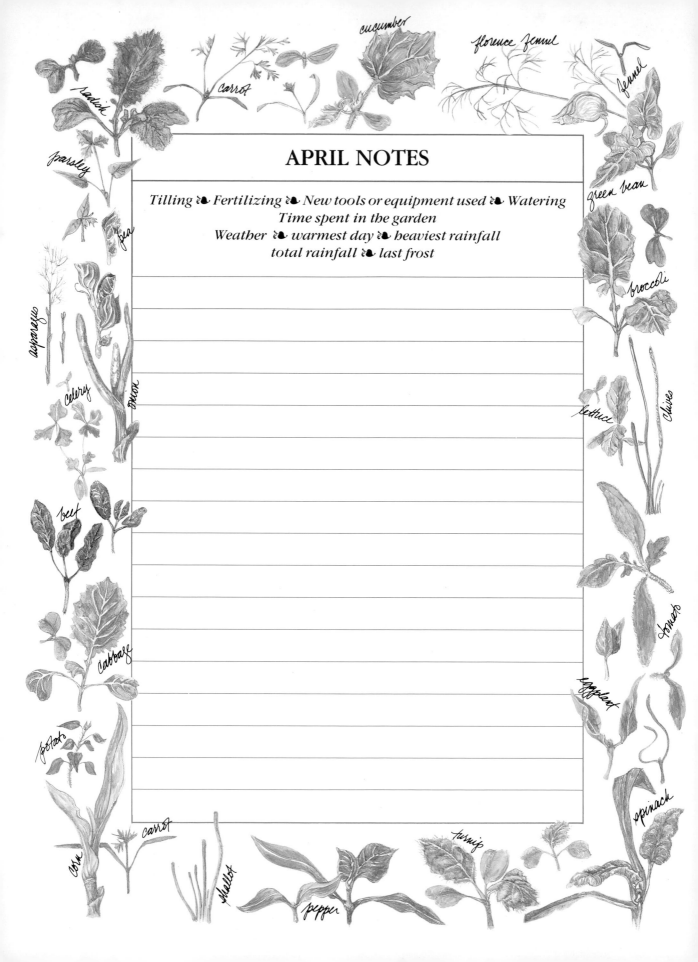

APRIL NOTES

Tilling ❧ Fertilizing ❧ New tools or equipment used ❧ Watering
Time spent in the garden
Weather ❧ warmest day ❧ heaviest rainfall
total rainfall ❧ last frost

APRIL NOTES

Oh thrice and four times happy those who plant cabbages!

—FRANÇOIS RABELAIS

Taraxacum officinale

MAY
MULCHING

As the days lengthen and the earth warms up, the first harvest arrives gloriously in the vegetable garden: such cool-season crops as lettuce, spinach, and radishes should be up and ready for admiring and eating. (For some thoughts on picking, see September.) Others may accompany them or follow close behind. Meanwhile, the planting goes on, for the garden is not likely to be working fully even by now. Depending on your climate, you may be sowing tender crops like lima beans as late as June. In May, however, most of the warm-season crops can go safely into the ground. And some crops previously set out may be so ebullient as to need thinning.

Along with all the planting, transplanting, and thinning come the first big maintenance chores. As soon as seedlings appear, the soil surrounding them should be cultivated, its surface broken up or at least scratched so that water will pass through readily. Cultivating should be repeated every week or so. An admittedly unexciting task, it nevertheless has the extra advantage of uprooting or discouraging weeds, which otherwise—quite apart from their unsightliness—will compete for nourishment with your vegetables and thus diminish the harvest. Weeds that cannot be dislodged with a hoe or cultivating tool must perforce be pulled by hand.

One good way to minimize weeds, if not to prevent them, is to apply a mulch around each row or patch. By shading the soil, mulches inhibit weed growth; at the same time they keep the ground from drying out and help moderate the soil's temperature. They also prevent erosion while keeping the soil loose and open. Most mulches are applied in late spring, after seedlings are up and the soil has warmed, although some gardeners insist they are better off keeping mulch on the ground all year long; they pull the mulch away from the rows in March or April when planting, then pull it back in place later when the ground has warmed.

Mulches can be made of many diverse substances—mulch hay, pine needles, and even grass clippings have their enthusiasts (but be careful not to use clippings from a lawn treated within three weeks with a herbicide). In a

shepherd's purse

51

special category is black plastic sheeting. Although some are offended by its looks, it is especially valuable in northern climates as it very efficiently warms the top soil layer in early spring, permitting earlier planting. Then, having performed its warming service, it proceeds to cool the soil during the summer. One proviso: it must be anchored, either with stones or by burying its edges, or it will blow away.

Another fine mulch is compost. Rich in microorganisms, it works not just as a mulch but as a soil conditioner (rivaling peat moss in this respect, and certainly beating it on cost) and a fertilizer. Constructing a compost pile need not be difficult (see page 54), and no self-respecting gardener should dismiss the possibility of having one.

common knotgrass

carpetweed

wild mustard

lamb's quarters

CHECKLIST FOR MAY

☐ Plant and transplant

☐ Cultivate

☐ Weed

☐ Thin as needed

☐ Apply mulch

☐ Fertilize and side dress as needed

☐ Water

☐ Continue pest management

☐ Harvest first crops

SOIL TEMPERATURE

In most cases, mulch should not be applied until the soil has warmed sufficiently. A reading of 60°F or so should be acceptable. The temperature can be taken simply by taking an ordinary outdoor thermometer and plunging it in the soil.

purslane   prickly lettuce

SALT HAY VS. MULCH HAY

Two kinds of hay are sold as mulch. Salt hay—also called salt marsh hay—is a slow-rotting hay cut from saline areas near the seashore. Because of its salt content, it does not introduce weed seeds into normal garden soil, and many gardeners consider it the best mulch. Nevertheless, it is expensive and hard to find in regions far from the shore. Mulch hay—also called old or spoiled hay—is ordinary field hay that a farmer has declared surplus (or that was rained on). Because it breaks down relatively quickly and is cheaper, its partisans deem it superior to its salty cousin (overlooking its tendency to foster weeds), and some use it as a permanent mulch, keeping it in place throughout the year except at planting time and merely adding to it as needed.

THE COMPOST PILE

Constructing a compost pile is sometimes postulated as a highly elaborate undertaking, involving many discrete layers and the addition of various activators and other substances, but it does not have to be so complex. Most gardeners feel it makes sense, however, to maintain three separate but adjoining piles: one that is receiving new materials, a second that is "cooking," or preparing itself, and a third that is being used. Ideally, the piles should be enclosed in fences or perforated walls (like concrete blocks with open spaces interspersed) so that air can circulate readily, but simple heaps on the ground will also serve. Any organic refuse that comes from the kitchen (except fats) or garden (except weeds gone to seed) can be added to the pile and in virtually any order. (At the end of the season some gardeners add spent plants, but it's advisable not to add bean plants; bean beetles have a remarkable ability to overwinter in the pile.) Decay will be hastened if the two piles in preparation—the first and second ones—are turned now and then to mix the ingredients, and a pile's top should be shaped so that it will collect rainwater. The compost is ready for use when it has become crumbly and dark brown.

WATERING NEEDS

Most gardens should receive at least 1 inch of water a week. If nature provides it, fine. If not, the gardener must do so. To measure precipitation, you can use a rain gauge or any similar container, even a coffee can. (For a more detailed discussion of watering, see August.)

CONTROLLING WEEDS

Every gardener knows the adage, "A weed is a plant out of place." So in the vegetable garden any plant other than what you wish to raise is a weed. Some plants commonly thought of as weeds may even be worth growing for their own sake—amaranth (also known as red-root, wild beet, or pigweed), lamb's quarters (also known as goosefoot or wild spinach), and dandelion, for example; all are tasty and nutritious. Most other extraneous plants must be suppressed or removed lest they compete with your crops.

Distinguishing weeds from the vegetables you have planted may be difficult when the first shoots appear. Knowing how the vegetable seedlings themselves look (see the borders in April) may help. If you have planted seeds in a straight row you can assume everything not in the row is a weed. In a widely-planted row it is usually safe to say that the largest number of seedlings of the same type are the ones worth saving.

To some extent weeds can be controlled through the use of herbicides, but such substances should be used with extreme caution as they can also destroy your vegetables: read the label carefully. In any case, avoid hormone-type herbicides such as 2,4-D. Most vegetable gardeners resort to any one (or all) of three tried-and-true methods:

Cultivating. Breaking up the soil's surface to a depth of not more than half an inch keeps most weeds from gaining a foothold.

Mulching. Covering the soil will suffocate unwanted growths, depriving them of light. Black pastic is especially recommended as a weed eradicator.

Pulling by hand. The most effective technique, and necessary when a weed appears right next to a vegetable, it is also the most difficult and time-consuming. At the season's height it may be needed at least once a week. The chore is easiest when the weed is small and after a rain, when the soil is moist and roots come up easily.

PEST AND DISEASE CONTROL

DATE	SYMPTOM	CONTROL	WHERE AND HOW APPLIED	RESULTS

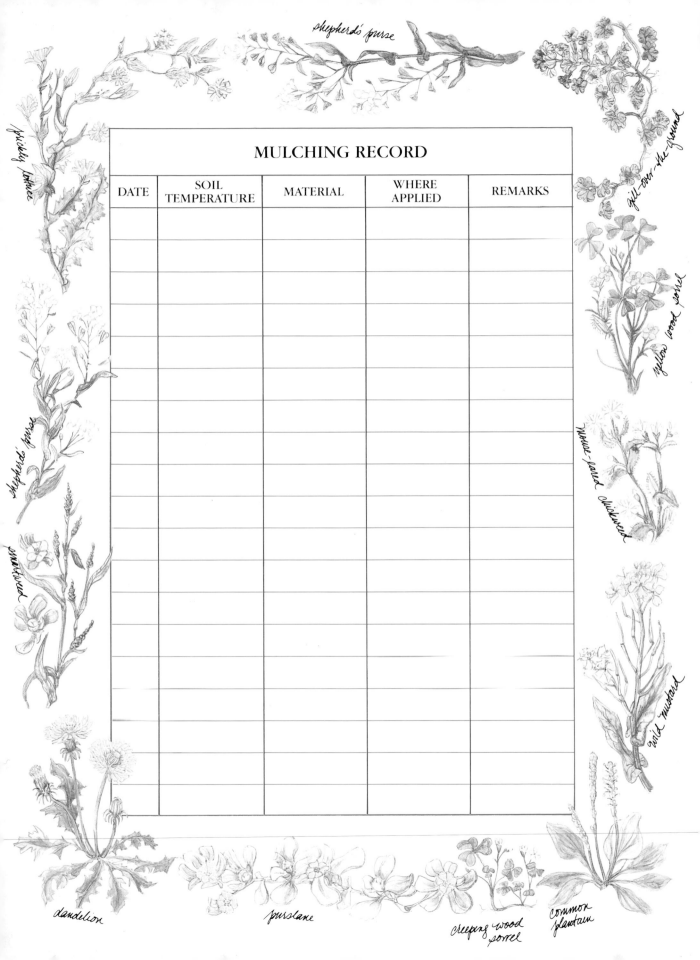

MULCHING RECORD

DATE	SOIL TEMPERATURE	MATERIAL	WHERE APPLIED	REMARKS

shepherd's purse

prickly lettuce

gill-over-the-ground

yellow wood sorrel

shepherd's purse

mouse-eared chickweed

smartweed

wild mustard

dandelion

purslane

creeping wood sorrel

common plantain

MAY NOTES

Cultivating ❧ Thinning ❧ Weeding ❧ Watering
Fertilizing and side dressing ❧ Time spent in the garden
Weather ❧ rainfall for month

MAY NOTES

A careful Gard'ner in this Month will be sure to do what he left undone in April.

—FRANCIS GENTIL-LOUIS LIGER D'AUXERRE

Brassica botrytis

JUNE
ROTATING CROPS

The month of June over much of the U.S. witnesses a shift in the vegetable garden. Many of the first crops planted will now be delivering substantial yields or may even have finished producing, and the time will have arrived to re- place them with others to keep the garden fully engaged. Thus you will be putting into effect the process known as succession planting or double-cropping that was first envisioned in January when the garden was planned. Cool-season vegetables like peas and radishes can be pulled up, their places taken by crops that thrive in the summer (like cucumbers or bush beans) or even by those that can start now but mature only in the fall (like pumpkins). The replacing and shifting continues for most of the summer as harvests occur, and you should keep track of these activities in the record of planting at the end of the book.

A number of options present themselves. You may expand your planting of a crop already started, adding a row or two. Or you may begin an entirely new crop, like summer squash or—if you have not previously done so and have room for it—corn. You may even decide to introduce a bit of extra color and variety into the garden by abandoning vegetables in a few spots and planting annual flowers like nasturtiums or petunias or zinnias.

One other possibility is worth consideration, particularly in larger gardens. That is to take the row or patch out of vegetable or flower production and plant a cover crop, one that will help the soil to rest and renew itself. Known as green manures because they provide valuable nourishment, cover crops like buckwheat, rye, oats, or clover also im- prove soil texture. And they encourage earthworms. Green manures are a good choice especially in spots where the garden has been intensively cultivated over the past few years. Next spring you can turn them under and start a new vegetable crop.

If you are replacing one vegetable crop with another, it is a good idea to practice rotation by choosing one that makes different demands on the soil. In any event, be sure to fertilize again—the first crop will surely have depleted the soil's nutrients, especially if the soil is sandy. As you did in January, check the number of days to maturity for each planting: in the near run you will want to avoid starting a crop that would be ready for harvesting when you are away on vacation, and in the longer view you will want to make sure the harvest occurs before the autumnal frost. Aside from the cole crops, few vegetables are able to survive the first good sub-freezing temperatures in the fall. Your County Agent can verify the expected first frost date for your area. For a list of frost-resistant crops, see October.

CHECKLIST FOR JUNE

☐ Review the plan of your garden

☐ Plant and transplant

☐ Cultivate

☐ Water

☐ Start succession planting

☐ Fertilize and side dress as needed

☐ Continue pest management

☐ Weed

☐ Harvest early crops

SUCCESSION CROPS

The following are plants that mature early and may either be resown to produce a follow-up harvest or used to replace other crops: bush beans, beets, cabbage, carrots, radishes, kohlrabi, endive, broccoli. Turnips can be sown in July; lettuce in August.

Plants that mature later on in the season but can be planted now: corn, cucumbers, okra, kale, rutabaga, summer squash, oriental radishes.

PEST AND DISEASE CONTROL

DATE	SYMPTOM	CONTROL	WHERE AND HOW APPLIED	RESULTS

JUNE NOTES

*Cultivating ❧ Thinning ❧ Weeding ❧ Fertilizing and side
dressing ❧ Watering ❧ Time spent in the garden
Weather ❧ rainfall this month ❧ high temperature*

JUNE NOTES

Come into the garden, Maud.

—Alfred, Lord Tennyson

But don't go into Mr. McGregor's garden.

—Beatrix Potter

PESTS AND DISEASES

Lycopersicon lycopersicum

With the summer's heat comes a welcome series of harvests in most gardens: beans, beets, and broccoli among others will continue to come in during July; the first corn may be ready; and tomato plants may begin producing. But with the bounty may also come an increase in some problems encountered earlier, as undesired creatures and ailments are found marring the bucolic scene with renewed vigor. It is wise to be vigilant toward pests and diseases from the very beginning of the season; in the midsummer weeks it becomes mandatory.

While insects and other small marauders are inevitable, they can be readily controlled if identified and dealt with early. Professionals urge a program that they call pest management: prevent insects if you can, but otherwise be content to minimize their effect. The occasional beetle or large worm (like the giant tomato hornworm) can be picked off manually; aphids and spider mites can usually be flushed off with a water spray. Some invaders may seem to require more severe remedies, but it is best to avoid potent insecticides as they can not only injure your crops but often harm you as well. Many gardeners achieve success using so-called natural or biological insecticides—like rotenone or Bacillus thuringiensis, both made from plant substances—which can control some predatory insects but are safe for humans if used properly. Powerful chemicals like malathion and diazinon are highly effective, but they should be used according to label directions and only when needed (see the charts that follow).

Insect control can in turn help mitigate the onset of diseases, as many ailments are spread by pests. But the best way to keep plant diseases to a minimum is to keep the garden as a whole clean and healthy. Buy treated seeds (ones processed with a fungicide) and make sure all purchased transplants are disease-free. Rotate crops from one year to the next; keep your soil well-tilled and well-drained; keep the garden free of refuse, weeds, and dead plants; water early in the day to allow soil to dry by nightfall; inspect all plants carefully at least once a week for signs of infestation; and eliminate diseased plants immediately. Spraying with fungicides can help contain diseases that have already taken hold, but a diseased plant can rarely be brought back to health. The only real defense is prevention. And it must also be admitted, finally, that some diseases are weather-related, and these diseases may show up despite all preventive efforts.

A third threat, especially in suburban and rural gardens, is represented by animals and birds that wish to partake of your vegetables before you do. A good chicken-wire fence should keep rabbits and woodchucks out, but electrified wires may be needed against raccoons and deer. Live animal traps, which enclose the intruder harmlessly in a screened device, can be useful—the captured animal can be released miles away. Bird netting can protect corn and other seedlings; birds may also be scared away by fake owls or shiny hanging objects that move in the wind. And while some gardeners continue to swear by that old standby, the scarecrow, others rely on a more modern remedy—tuning an inexpensive radio to a talk show and setting it in the garden.

Remember that it is by no means too late to plant new crops as harvests are completed. The season has many weeks to go in most areas, and in that time many vegetables can be planted, raised, and brought in to the table. July is also a good time to start thinking about preserving any excess crops; for more information about canning and other methods, see September.

CHECKLIST FOR JULY

☐ Continue succession planting

☐ Cultivate

☐ Water

☐ Weed

☐ Fertilize and side dress as needed

☐ Continue pest management

☐ Harvest

☐ Preserve surplus harvest

PEST AND DISEASE CONTROL				
DATE	SYMPTOM	CONTROL	WHERE AND HOW APPLIED	RESULTS

SOME COMMON DISEASES

AILMENT	MANIFESTATION	PREVENTION
Blossom-end rot	Dry, leathery, blackened ends of tomatoes or peppers	Water transplants regularly, mulch young plants, add limestone to soil if pH is low
Fusarium and verticillium wilts	Fungus disease causing tomato, pepper, potato, and eggplant plants to wilt and die	Rotate crops, grow resistant varieties
Leaf blights and spots	Fungus spotting leaves of beans, beets, cucumbers, eggplant, potatoes, tomatoes	Rotate crops, spray with fungicide
Mildew	White or brown growth on leaves of beans, cucumbers, squash, pumpkins	Use resistant varieties and appropriate fungicide, rotate crops
Nematodes	Microscopic wormlike creatures cause stunting of tomatoes, cucumbers, and other plants	Rotate crops; planting marigolds nearby may help
Viruses	Yellowing, stunting, or spotting of various vegetables	Use resistant varieties, control weeds and aphids

SOME COMMON PESTS

PEST	APPEARANCE AND EFFECT	REMEDY
Aphids	Tiny green (or red or black) licelike bugs suck sap from shoots of cabbage-type plants especially and many others	Douse with water or spray with rotenone; if ineffective, try malathion
Cabbage maggots	Tiny white worms underground cause wilting of cabbages and similar crops	Spray with diazinon or lay down maggot mats, tar paper, or foil around stems
Cabbage worm caterpillars	1-inch-long crawlers chew holes in cabbage leaves and heads	Spray with Bacillus thuringiensis or rotenone

PEST	APPEARANCE AND EFFECT	REMEDY
Corn earworms	2-inch caterpillars eat corn kernels, tomatoes, peppers	Spray with rotenone
Cucumber beetles	Bugs with three stripes down their backs feed on young cucumbers	Spray with rotenone or pyrethrum
Cutworms	Caterpillarlike creatures eat stems of young cabbages and other seedlings	Install paper collar around seedling stem
Japanese beetles	Half-inch-long green and brown bugs attack leaves and flowers of many plants	Install beetle trap (available at garden centers) or spray with carbaryl
Leaf miners	Grublike creatures burrow through leaves of many vegetables	Spray with pyrethrum, diazinon, or malathion
Mexican bean beetles	Resemble ladybugs but have sixteen spots on back; eat leaves and beans of bean crops	Spray with rotenone, diazinon, or malathion
Potato bugs (Colorado potato beetle)	Striped bugs lay orange eggs on underside of potato leaves; offspring can destroy potato, tomato, eggplant, and other plants	Pick off or spray with rotenone or malathion
Spider mites	Tiny red or white mites suck plant juices	Douse with water or use a proven miticide
Slugs	Slimy worms feed on leaves at night	Pick off or trap with beer in saucer on ground
Stalk borers (several kinds)	Eat holes in stalk of squash and other plants, then devour stalk's insides	Eliminate weeds where they breed; spray with carbaryl
Tomato hornworms	3-inch-long worms feed on tomato leaves	Pick off or spray with Bacillus thuringiensis
Whiteflies	Tiny, mothlike flies suck juices from undersides of leaves	Spray with rotenone or pyrethrum

COMPANION PLANTING FOR INSECT CONTROL

*Organic gardeners in particular put great store in the presumed
ability of certain plants, because of their aroma or for other reasons, to
suppress or inhibit harmful insects. As enumerated by Louise Riotte in*
Secrets of Companion Planting, *the following plants may be effective:*

Dead nettle against potato bugs

Garlic against Japanese beetles, aphids, and spider mites

Horseradish against potato bugs

Marigolds against nematodes, Mexican bean beetles, and other insects

Nasturtiums against aphids, squash bugs, and pumpkin beetles

Petunias against many beetles

Rosemary against cabbage moths, bean beetles, and carrot flies

Rue against Japanese beetles

Spearmint against ants and aphids

Summer savory against bean beetles

Tansy against Japanese beetles, cucumber beetles, and squash bugs

Thyme against cabbage worms

White geraniums against Japanese beetles

Wormwood against cabbage worm butterflies and black flea beetles

BENEFICIAL INSECTS

At least four kinds of predatory insects are valued by many gardeners as they prey on creatures that are harmful to plants. Ladybugs devour aphids and other soft-bodied insects; praying mantises feed on large pests like grasshoppers; lacewings eat both aphids and spider mites; braconid wasps lay eggs on large worms (like the tomato hornworm), and the resulting larvae devour their host. But both ladybugs and lacewings require a steady food supply or they will depart; the mantis as well as other such creatures may eat other beneficial insects as well as harmful ones. It is unwise to rely solely on such creatures to rid the garden of pests.

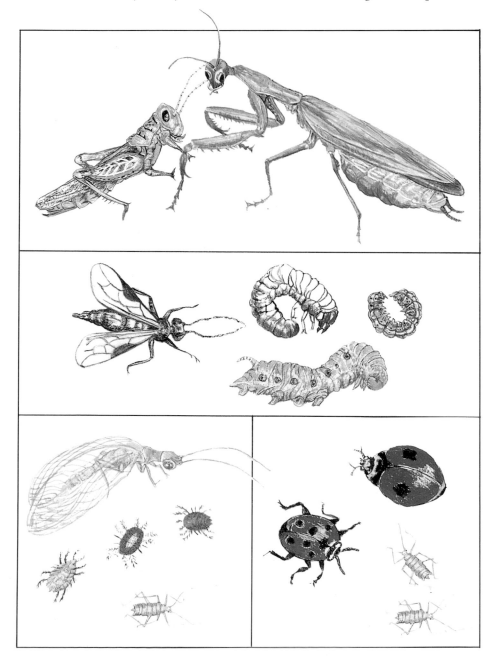

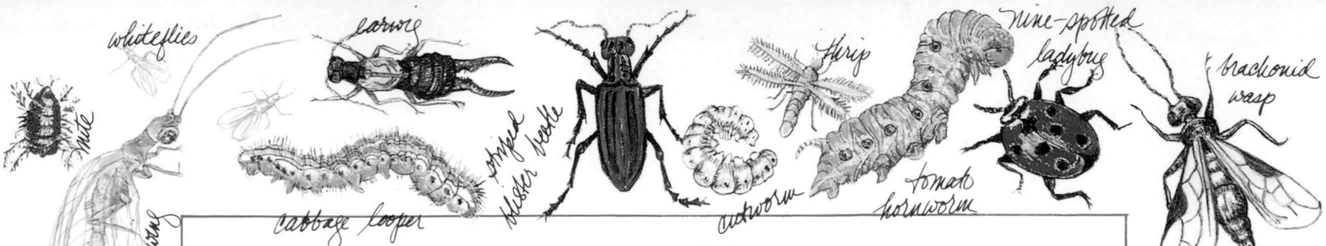

JULY NOTES

Cultivating ❧ Weeding ❧ Fertilizing and side dressing
Watering ❧ Time spent in the garden
Problems encountered thus far ❧ Adjustments to consider
Weather

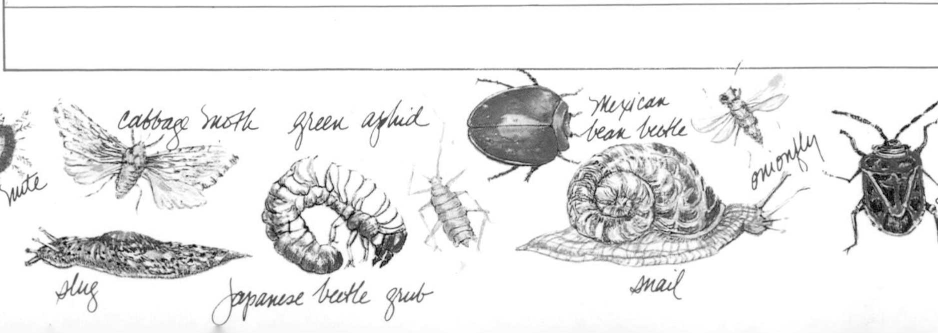

whiteflies

earwig

thrip

nine-spotted ladybug

brachonid wasp

mite

oriental blister beetle

cabbage looper

cutworm

tomato hornworm

mite

symphylan

mite

whiteflies

diamondback moth

green shield bug

sow bug

imported cabbage worm

Mexican bean beetle

Eastern wireworm

striped cucumber beetle

leafhopper

two-spotted ladybug

Colorado potato beetle

melon thrip

praying mantis

cutworm

differential grasshopper

mite

cabbage moth

green aphid

Mexican bean beetle

onionfly

harlequin cabbage bug

slug

Japanese beetle grub

snail

JULY NOTES

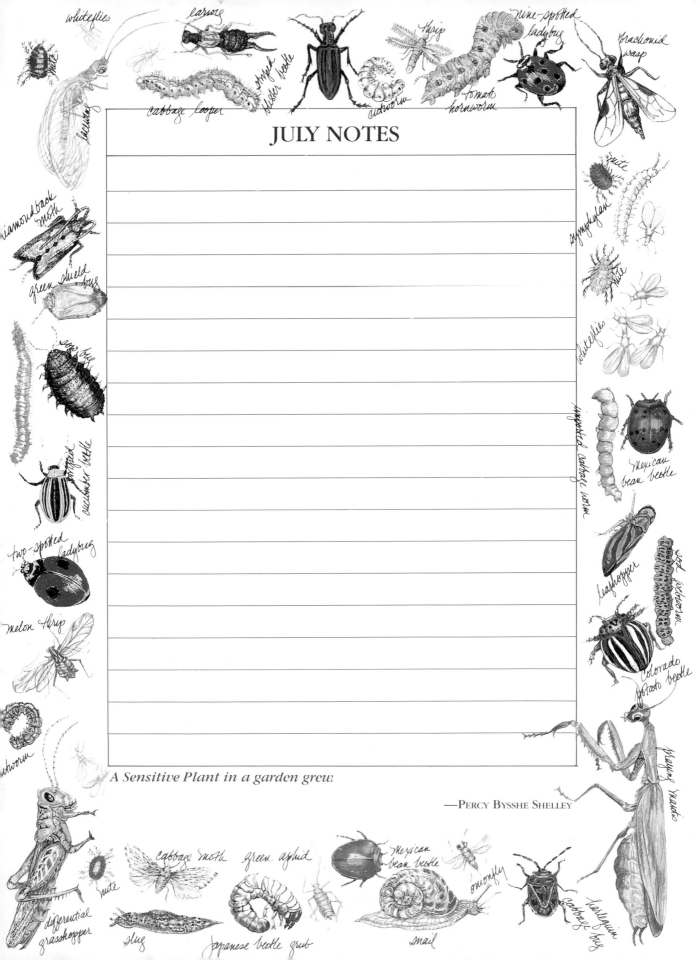

A Sensitive Plant in a garden grew.

—Percy Bysshe Shelley

WATERING

Throughout the summer months the gardener is reminded how vital proper watering is. Heat can dry out plants at a rapid rate, and the soil can suddenly seem arid, threatening everything there. So it cannot hurt for an experienced gardener to review some of the principles governing what is otherwise an almost routine chore.

The key dictum is to water when rainfall is inadequate. Under normal circumstances most vegetable gardens should receive the equivalent of 1 inch of water per week, either in rainfall or via watering; an empty can placed in the open will reveal how much rain has fallen. Additional watering will be needed, of course, during a heat wave. And vegetables that produce fruit or set pods—like peas, beans, corn, and tomatoes—require extra moisture when they are flowering or setting their fruit or pods. Leaf crops and root crops simply need water on a steady basis.

When you do water, make sure the soil is cultivated well enough to receive it without runoff, and apply enough to wet the soil to a depth of at least 6 to 8 inches (you may want to dig a test hole or two to check); watering the surface alone encourages plants to develop shallow roots, which are weak. But do not overwater. All plants require air as well as moisture, and soggy soil can foment root rot by depriving the roots of needed oxygen. Note that sandy soils absorb moisture rapidly but dissipate it equally fast; clay soils take on water slowly but retain it almost too well. If a soil's high clay content leads to drainage problems, consider mounding up the soil when you plant: raised beds generally drain efficiently. Then plan to lighten the soil the next time you recondition the garden (see November).

As to the many ways in which water can be applied, sprinkling by hand is often the least effective, for gauging how much you have put down and where is extremely difficult. Oscillating sprinklers, which move back and forth to cover a rectangular space, are better than rotary ones, which tend to distribute the water too rapidly for the ground to absorb. Impact sprinklers, those pulsating devices that can be set to blanket any designated area, may be the best as they can be adjusted exactly. One drawback to any sprinkler is its tendency to lose water through evaporation; another is that much of its water goes on the leaves, whereas it is the roots that need moisture. Two methods circumvent that dilemma. One is furrow irrigation: if your garden has a slight slope you can run water between the rows, either letting the water flow along the ground itself or running it through troughs into which holes have been drilled to distribute the moisture evenly. The other is drip watering, usually accomplished by means of a soaker hose or perforated plastic

tube that emits the water in driblets over a long period. Both furrow and drip watering have the advantage of applying the water directly to the plant roots, where it's needed.

Some gardeners deliberately underwater at times to provoke plants into production. Such "water stress" can, for example, jolt a tomato plant into ripening its fruit. For most vegetable growers, however, underwatering is much too risky: it can cut the yield and quality of an entire crop. It's better to provide adequate moisture at all times to bring the garden safely through the warm season. If constant watering is impractical, be sure to water as outlined above—in the morning, and thoroughly.

CHECKLIST FOR AUGUST

☐ Review watering methods

☐ Continue succession planting

☐ Cultivate

☐ Weed

☐ Fertilize and side dress as needed

☐ Continue pest management

☐ Harvest

☐ Preserve surplus harvest

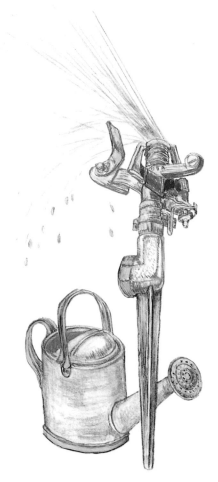

PEST AND DISEASE CONTROL

DATE	SYMPTOM	CONTROL	WHERE AND HOW APPLIED	RESULTS

AUGUST NOTES

Weeding  Side dressing  Cultivating  Watering
Time spent in the garden
Problems  Quality of harvest thus far
Weather

AUGUST NOTES

Nine bean-rows will I have there...

—William Butler Yeats

Beta vulgaris

THE HARVEST

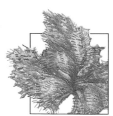

As the season moves along, the vegetable gardener can be forgiven for thinking more and more about the total return from the growing area, the cumulation of all the harvests. By early September plans for another (and better) year are probably beginning to take shape, the result of observations of how this year's crops have turned out. It is not too early to jot down a few notes on how certain vegetables did, what might be adjusted next year, and what problems were solved—or not—to your satisfaction.

September is in many regions the culminating harvest month, even though plenty of crops will still be producing in October. Not only are the warm-season crops still flourishing, but some of the cool-season crops—planted in midsummer for fall harvesting—may be ready starting midway in the month. It is thus well to recall some tried and true notions governing the picking of vegetables. One is to pick young: vegetables are likely to be at their tastiest just before they have reached maturity, and may also contain more vitamins than they will later on. Second, to the extent possible, pick frequently and repeatedly, for in many cases leaving a crop unpicked will slow its development of new fruits and foliage. This is true particularly of leaf lettuce, which can yield three or four harvests before ceasing, but it is also the case with cucumbers, zucchini, peppers, and beans. Only a few vegetables, tomatoes for example, benefit from lingering on the vine. A third bit of advice is to pick vegetables as close as possible to the time of preparation and eating; furthermore, most vegetables will taste best if picked at the end of a clear, sunny day. The exceptions are lettuce, other leafy vegetables, and herbs, which are best gathered in the cool of the morning.

If you have picked more than you can consume, either inadvertently or by design, you will have been pondering the various ways of preserving what you have grown. Although it is not practicable here to describe the various techniques in detail, the main considerations involved in choosing between them can be summed up. Canning is the most exacting and time-consuming of the methods but does allow for ease of storage: the amount you can put up is limited only by your shelf space.

Canning's ramifications—relishes, preserves, and so on—also invite creativity. Freezing is relatively simple—follow the directions given in most good cookbooks for each freezable vegetable—but remember that you can only put up what you have room for in the freezer (whose electricity expense is another factor). The process of storing vegetables, putting them aside in a cool cellar or a warm-dry storage area, is almost as simple as freezing as most need only to be "cured" by warming in the sun; however, the number of crops that can readily be stored is limited. Leeks and some root crops, on the other hand, can be stored in the ground itself: if the soil is well mulched, the vegetables (carrots, onions, parsnips) can often be left there for several months, and some can stand a solid freeze. A final technique is drying, traditionally practiced with herbs but surprisingly effective with many vegetables—corn, for example.

A cautionary note for the end of summer: ease up on both watering and fertilizing. With only a few weeks remaining in the growing season, it makes sense to avoid encouraging crops too much; extra or undue blossoming or bearing runs the risk of being wiped out by the first frost.

CHECKLIST FOR SEPTEMBER

☐ General review of season

☐ Plant final crops

☐ Cultivate

☐ Water when necessary

☐ Weed

☐ Fertilize and side dress (only when necessary)

☐ Continue pest management

☐ Harvest

☐ Preserve surplus harvest

PEST AND DISEASE CONTROL				
DATE	SYMPTOM	CONTROL	WHERE AND HOW APPLIED	RESULTS

VEGETABLE YIELDS

According to the U.S. Department of Agriculture, the following yields can be expected, on the average, in a single 100-foot row planted to the vegetable designated. For shorter rows, divide the figure appropriately.

Asparagus	30	lb.	Lettuce, leaf	50	lb.
Beans, lima bush	25	lb. shelled	Muskmelon (cantalope)	100	fruits
Beans, lima pole	50	lb. shelled	Mustard	100	lb.
			Okra	100	lb.
Beans, snap bush	120	lb.	Onions (plants or sets)	100	lb.
Beans, snap pole	150	lb.			
Beets	150	lb.	Parsley	30	lb.
Broccoli	100	lb.	Parsnips	100	lb.
Brussels sprouts	75	lb.	Peas, English	20	lb.
Cabbage	150	lb.	Peas, southern	40	lb
Carrots	100	lb.	Peppers	60	lb.
Cauliflower	100	lb.	Potatoes	100	lb.
Celery	180	stalks	Pumpkins	100	lb.
Collards and kale	100	lb.	Radishes	100	bunches
Corn	120	ears	Spinach	40–50	lb.
Cucumbers	120	lb.	Squash, summer	150	lb.
Eggplant	100	lb.	Squash, winter	100	lb.
Garlic	40	lb.	Tomatoes	100	lb.
Kohlrabi	75	lb.	Turnips	50–100	lb.
Lettuce, head	100	heads	Watermelons	40	fruits

SOME VEGETABLES FOR CANNING

Note: Many books on canning and other preserving techniques provide copious information on the subject. You would be wise to read them, not only for instructions but for recipes for a great variety of pickles, relishes, butters, and the like.

Asparagus	Carrots	Peppers
Beans, lima	Corn	Potatoes
Beans, snap	Eggplant	Pumpkins
Beets	Greens	Squash, summer
	Peas	Tomatoes

SOME VEGETABLES FOR FREEZING

Asparagus	Cauliflower	Peas
Beans, lima	Corn	Peppers
Beans, snap	Eggplant	Sweet potatoes
Beets	Greens	Pumpkins
Broccoli	Kohlrabi	Squash
Brussels sprouts	Okra	Tomatoes
Cabbage	Onions	Turnips
Carrots		

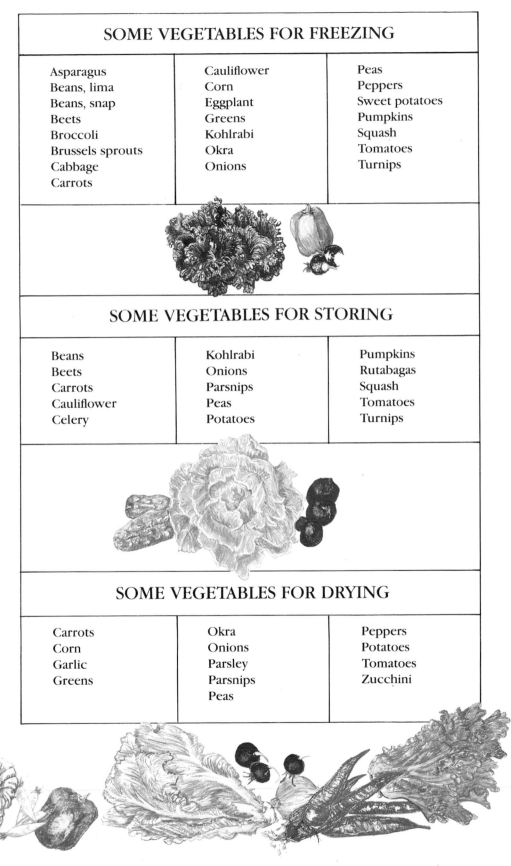

SOME VEGETABLES FOR STORING

Beans	Kohlrabi	Pumpkins
Beets	Onions	Rutabagas
Carrots	Parsnips	Squash
Cauliflower	Peas	Tomatoes
Celery	Potatoes	Turnips

SOME VEGETABLES FOR DRYING

Carrots	Okra	Peppers
Corn	Onions	Potatoes
Garlic	Parsley	Tomatoes
Greens	Parsnips	Zucchini
	Peas	

SEPTEMBER NOTES

Fertilizing and side dressing ❧ *Watering* ❧ *Weeding*
Time spent in the garden ❧ *Crop review*
Weather

SEPTEMBER NOTES

It was as true… as turnips is.

—Charles Dickens

LATE-SEASON CROPS

The days get shorter, the first cold winds blow across the garden, and for many vegetable growers the time will have come to close down. Resourceful practitioners, however, if they planted fall crops during the summer months, will continue—weather permitting—to gather in the garden's bounty. Potatoes can often be dug until well along in the month; tomatoes may also be available until frost; and most of the cabbage family will go on bearing, seemingly unaffected by dropping temperatures. So will root crops such as carrots. Some crops, notably Brussels sprouts, are actually improved by the first frost and can be harvested almost until the ground freezes solid.

A few tender crops that might otherwise be wiped out by a good frost can often be safeguarded through the judicious use of protective devices. So the coverings, hoods, and mulches that were invoked in the spring to save seedlings against a final cold snap can once again come into play. It is a good idea, a day or two before the first sub freezing temperatures are likely to arrive (a call to the County Agent can provide the best guidance as to specific dates in your area), to pick any of the tender vegetables that are ripe. The plants remaining thereafter can frequently be coaxed into further production if covered at night with tarpaulins, blankets, or plastic, or if well mulched, for example with salt hay. Be sure to remove any coverings in the morning if the weather promises to turn warm. Many gardeners find that the effects of a mild frost can be dispelled by spraying the garden at sunup with a fine mist, as the water will help warm the plant tissues; be sure to continue misting until the sun's warmth has melted any ice.

When a crop ceases production, it is wise to remove it from the garden, clearing the ground; residues can be added to the compost pile. Some growers, unless they expect to undertake a thorough soil reconditioning later in the fall (see November), plant cover crops in the vacated spaces. If started in time, a sowing of ryegrass will yield a good cover before winter sets in, and when spring arrives this green manure can be tilled under to provide added enrichment to the waiting beds. Alternatively, a few overwintering vegetable crops like garlic, scallions, or shallots can be planted now.

Brassica oleracea

CHECKLIST FOR OCTOBER

☐ Water and mist remaining crops

☐ Transplant to cold frame

☐ Harvest

☐ Preserve surplus

☐ Plant cover crops

☐ Clean up

PREDICTING FROSTS

Given the tricky nature of all weather predicting, it is usually very difficult to say just when a frost will occur. Newspaper and TV or radio reports can be misleading because they must perforce be based on a wide area that contains multitudes of microclimates—which can vary widely. Local papers and stations generally lack the resources to be any more exact. The best advice for gardeners is likely to come from the local County Agent, who not only is familiar with the immediate terrain, but is attuned to the specific problems and needs of both amateur and commercial gardeners in the area.

Aside from what the authorities predict, experienced gardeners know that certain conditions typically bring on frost. The weather will have been stormy but is now clearing, with the barometer rising and the temperature falling. Northerly winds have brought in cool air, but toward nightfall the wind drops. If the temperature at sunset is 40°F or lower, the likelihood of frost occurring some time before dawn is overwhelming.

LIGHT VS. HEAVY FROSTS

There is no clear dividing line between "light" and "heavy" frost conditions, but in theory a light frost is one that many otherwise vulnerable plants will survive, while a heavy one will most assuredly zap them. Although water freezes at temperatures below 32°F, the cold's effects may take some time to be manifested, and sometimes the thermometer can drop to 30 or 29°F without much damage occurring. So a drop of just a few degrees below freezing will generally be considered a light frost. What actually happens in a frost, botanists believe, is that ice crystals forming in and around a plant's cells act to dehydrate the plant, causing it in effect to die of thirst. "Hardy" plants are those whose tissues, because of complex adaptation processes in the past, are able to resist such injury. In a sense, however, there are no completely hardy plants, for all living things perish at some degree of coldness.

FROST RESISTANCE		
VEGETABLES THAT ENDURE LIGHT FROST	VEGETABLES IMPROVED BY LIGHT FROST	VEGETABLES THAT SURVIVE HEAVY FROST
Broccoli Brussels sprouts Cabbage Cauliflower Celery Collards Kale Leeks Lettuce Peas Radishes Spinach	Cabbage family Root crops	Leeks Root crops

OCTOBER NOTES

*Garden cleanups ❧ Time spent ❧ Frost protection
Weather ❧ date of first frost ❧ predicted low temperatures
❧ actual low temperatures*

OCTOBER NOTES

Let the onion flourish there,
Rose among roots, the maiden-fair,
Wine-scented and poetic soul
of the capacious salad bowl.

—ROBERT LEWIS STEVENSON

NOVEMBER
RECONDITIONING THE SOIL

Allium sativum

Allium cepa

 In the great campaign to achieve wondrous productivity in the garden, nothing is more important than reconditioning the soil in the fall, after all the crops are in. Many gardeners take care of this chore in November. (Some who do not, and justifiably, are those who maintain permanent mulches on their vegetable beds, for the mulch, if left in place, keeps the soil in a proper condition.) Although upgrading can also be done in the spring-time just before planting, autumn is better as it allows added ingredients a chance to work their way into the soil for maximum effectiveness. It also lightens the work load next spring. The task must be done yearly, as under normal circumstances the growing of crops inevitably drains the soil of essential nutrients and conditioning materials, which must be replaced. Sun, wind, and your footsteps also make for compacting, which must be alleviated. The ideal soil, as veterans know, is a fairly light loamy mix that is not too sandy or too much on the clay side and that is rich in humus. It must further have good moisture-holding capacity while draining well: water must reach the roots readily, but so must air. The perfect mix, teeming with microorganisms, can readily be attained through a little diligent work.

Before you proceed, it's a good idea to be sure the garden patch is totally clear of all stakes and other growing aids. Pull up trellises, fences, and labeling devices and set them aside for the winter. Plant residues can go on the compost pile unless there is a chance of their containing the remnants of insects or diseases, in which case they should be burned.

Now test the soil for its pH—the extent to which it is more acid or more alkaline—as this may have shifted during the year. The best soil for vegetables has a pH between 6.0 and 6.8 (see March). You can use your own testing kit or, for a more exact reading, send a sample to your County Agent for analysis. Then correct according to the Agent's (or the test kit's) recommendations, adding lime to push the soil toward alkalinity, or ground sulfur to heighten its acidity.

Next, add organic matter. Peat moss is perhaps the best, though it is expensive. Virtually as good is leaf mold, if you have it. Compost is highly beneficial, but many gardeners prefer to use it in the spring rather than in the fall as it acts also as a fertilizer. Well-rotted manure, available in dried form at garden centers, is another alternative, though similarly expensive. Inexpensive, but hard to find, is barnyard manure; if it is well-rotted it will not burn, but even if it is fresh it will have time during the winter to break down. Whichever material you use, get plenty of it; experts recommend that it contain at least 2 percent organic matter, and for this to benefit the soil adequately you will want to add 3 or 4 inches of it overall. A large order, but one well worth attempting.

If you have access to a mechanical rotary tiller, you can use it to mix the additives into the soil, tilling to a depth of about 12 inches. Lacking that, it will be necessary to dig it in by hand, if possible by double-digging (see the discussion that follows). As you till or spade, remove any weeds, roots, or stones.

Finally, level the site, then test again for pH (peat moss and other substances can increase the acidity) and if need be correct for it. The end result is a rich, loamy expanse primed to give next year's crops a good sendoff.

CHECKLIST FOR NOVEMBER

☐ Final harvest

☐ Figure total yields for the year (enter on page 116)

☐ Preserve surplus

☐ Clear the site

☐ Recondition the soil

Foeniculum vulgare

DOUBLE-DIGGING

1. Dig a trench 1 foot deep and 1 foot wide along one edge of the garden, and use a wheelbarrow to deposit the dug soil at the other end of the garden.

2. Loosen and turn over the soil at the base of the trench, using a fork or spade. If possible, work organic matter into this lower soil.

3. Dig a second trench next to the first, filling the first with the soil removed from the second. Turn soil at bottom of second trench.

4. Continue digging trenches until you have reached the other end of the garden. Fill the final trench with the soil from the first.

RECONDITIONING RECORD			
DATE	METHOD USED	ADDITIVE	COMMENTS

NOVEMBER NOTES

Site clearing

NOVEMBER NOTES

This used to be among my prayers—a piece of land not so very large, which would contain a garden.

—Horace

TOOLS AND EQUIPMENT

Brassica capitata

Bitter winds and snow flurries may make vegetable gardening seem a bit distant in December, but the end of the year is a good time to check over the tools and equipment that can make all the difference in dispatching garden chores. The tools you already own should be cleaned, repaired, and put in good order; those you do not possess may often be purchased more economically in the off-season—and may make attractive gifts at holiday time.

What you need will of course depend on the size of your undertaking. Every vegetable grower, however, can probably agree on the essentials: a square-ended spade for cleaving tough soil and for basic digging and tilling, a long-handled shovel for moving and distributing various substances like peat moss and compost, a spading fork for loosening compacted soil and turning it over, a hoe for rough cultivating, an iron rake for leveling and smoothing, a trowel for planting, and a hand fork or small cultivator for close-in neatening of the planted rows. Plus a wheelbarrow or cart, surely a necessity for moving compost, lime, fertilizer, and the like.

Not quite so necessary but, in the opinion of many a gardener, very valuable even though somewhat expensive, are a number of other items: a shredder for cutting up garden and kitchen refuse to speed composting, a spreader for distributing fertilizers or lime evenly, some kind of shed to keep tools near the garden, and especially a mechanical rotary tiller. The best rotary tillers, which can cultivate lightly or dig deeply and turn over the earth to a depth of almost a foot, save not only time but your back muscles as well. (Be sure the tines are mounted behind the wheels rather than in front, so the wheels do not compact tilled soil.)

Occupying a middle ground between these two categories is a third group of gardening supplies ranging from sprinklers to seed-starting gadgetry: not absolutely essential but certainly useful. A checklist is on page 105.

In purchasing it is wise to get top quality, for well-made tools serve you better and last longer. Be a zealous maintainer: keep tools in good repair (tighten any loose handles) and well sharpened, oil moving parts as needed, and send out motorized items like a tiller for servicing as advised by the manufacturer. Read instruction labels carefully and observe all safety precautions. Do not leave gasoline in tanks over the winter.

As even the chilliest winter is bound to end, you may want to take advantage of the idle months to think about the coming year. Any reason to change crops or alter procedures that you adopted this year? Mistakes to correct? Problems still needing attention? Jot them down on pages 118–119. Finally, before the month is out be sure to send for seed catalogues if you are not already on the relevant mailing lists (for a list of seed companies, see February), and check with your County Agent for the latest word on new varieties and pesticide developments.

CHECKLIST FOR DECEMBER

☐   Review your year in the garden

☐   Check tools and equipment

☐   Repair and maintain tools

☐   Consider new purchases

☐   Order seed catalogues

☐   Send for latest Extension information

TOOL MAINTENANCE RECORD		
DATE	TOOL	REPAIR WORK DONE

TOOL AND EQUIPMENT CHECKLIST

BASIC TOOLS

Square-ended spade
Long-handled shovel
Spading fork
Hoe
Iron rake
Trowel
Small cultivator
Wheelbarrow or cart

MORE EXPENSIVE ITEMS

Shredder
Fertilizer spreader
Tool shed
Rotary tiller
Small tractor

MISCELLANEOUS SUPPLIES

SEED-STARTING

Peat pots
Peat pellets
Flats or trays
Soilless mix

SUPPORTS

Stakes, poles
Wire mesh or
  fencing
Lattice structures

WATERING

Hoses
Sprinklers
Soakers
Large watering
  can
Small watering
  can (for
  indoors)
Timer
Auxiliary shutoff
  valve
Drip attach-
  ments
Quick hose
  couplers

PEST AND DISEASE CONTROL

Sprayer, hand
Sprayer, back-
  pack
Sprayer, com-
  pressed-air
Sprayer, hose-
  attached
Duster, hand
Duster, plunger-
  type
Respirator or
  mask
Japanese beetle
  trap
Fencing
Electric wire
  fence

FROST PROTECTION

Cold frame
Plastic sheeting
Hot caps (covers
  for individual
  plants)

OTHER

Gloves
Knee pads
Planting board
Seeding aids
Row markers
Soil-test kit
Sifting screen
Rain gauge
Plastic mulch
Clippers
Shears
Jars for canning
Grow lights
Long-handled
  cultivator
Pitchfork
Iron bar (for
  moving rocks)
Post hole digger
Heart hoe (for
  making rows)
String
Edger

DECEMBER NOTES

Condition of stored vegetables 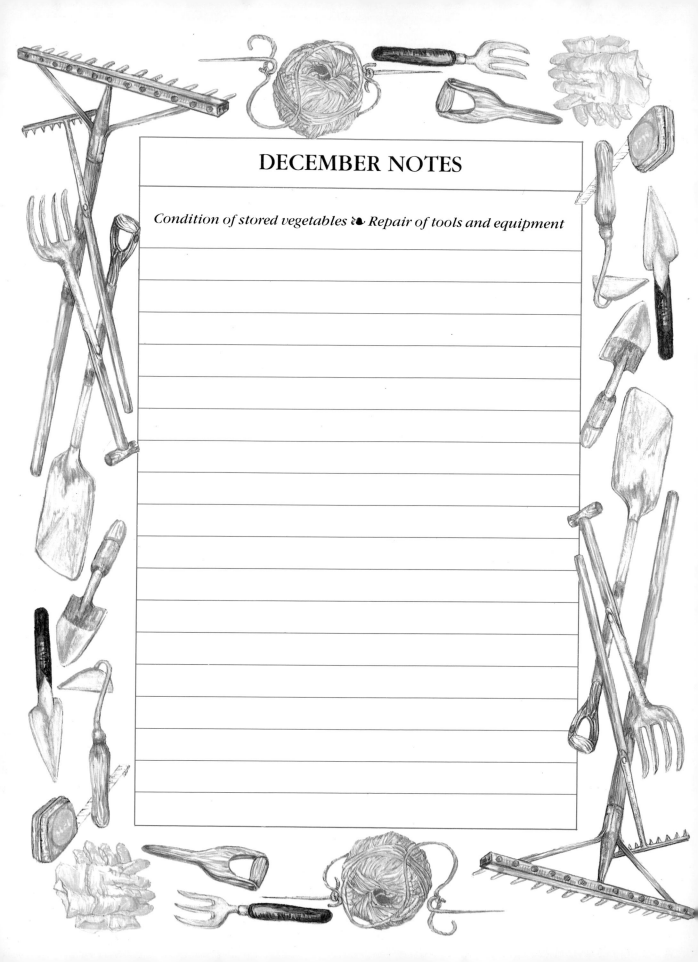 *Repair of tools and equipment*

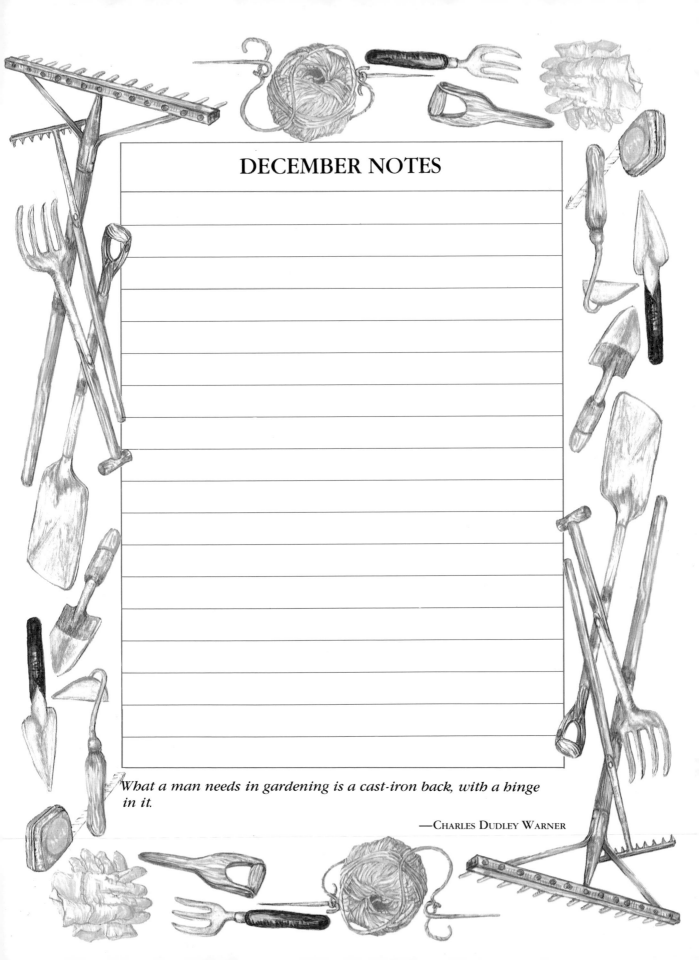

DECEMBER NOTES

What a man needs in gardening is a cast-iron back, with a hinge in it.

—CHARLES DUDLEY WARNER

A RECORD OF PLANTING

Enter all crops planted in the garden, either as seeds, transplants, or succession plantings.

DATE	CROP	SPACE OCCUPIED	SPROUTS NOTICED	FIRST FRUITING

A RECORD OF PLANTING

DATE	CROP	SPACE OCCUPIED	SPROUTS NOTICED	FIRST FRUITING

A RECORD OF PLANTING

DATE	CROP	SPACE OCCUPIED	SPROUTS NOTICED	FIRST FRUITING

A RECORD OF PLANTING

DATE	CROP	SPACE OCCUPIED	SPROUTS NOTICED	FIRST FRUITING
				green bean

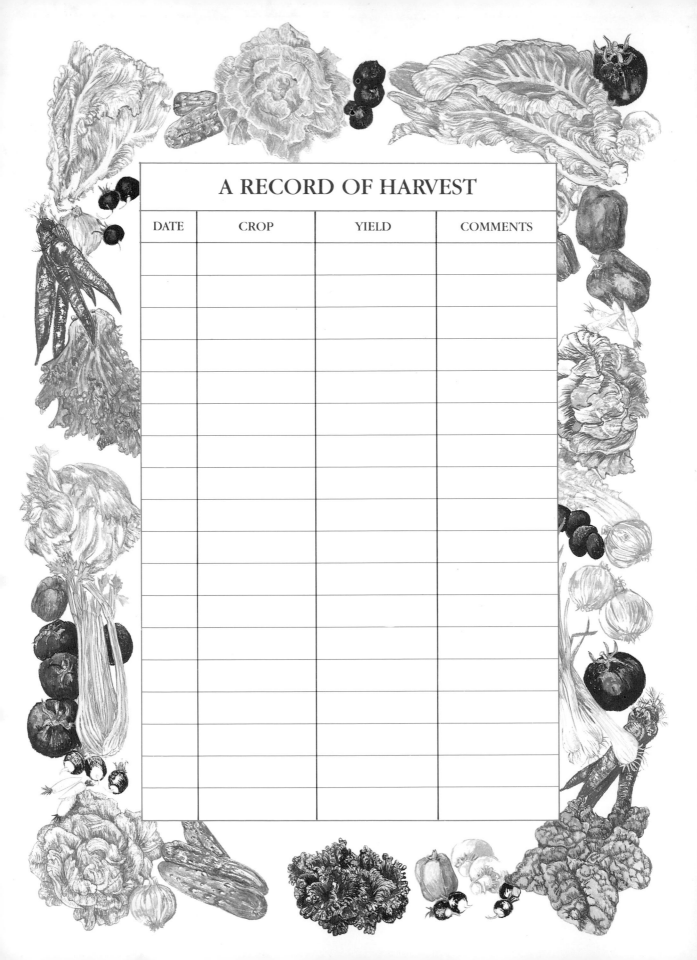

A RECORD OF HARVEST

DATE	CROP	YIELD	COMMENTS

A RECORD OF HARVEST

DATE	CROP	YIELD	COMMENTS

A RECORD OF HARVEST

DATE	CROP	YIELD	COMMENTS

A RECORD OF HARVEST

DATE	CROP	YIELD	COMMENTS

TOTAL YIELD

CROP	TOTAL YIELD

VEGETABLES PUT BY

DATE	VEGETABLE	HOW PRESERVED	AMOUNT

A REVIEW OF THE YEAR

Go back over your notes with an eye for possible changes in your gardening operation for next year.

CROPS RAISED	
TIMING OF CROPS	
SEED STARTING	
PLACEMENT	
AMOUNT GROWN	
FERTILIZERS	
MULCHES	
PEST AND DISEASE PROTECTION	
FROST PROTECTION	

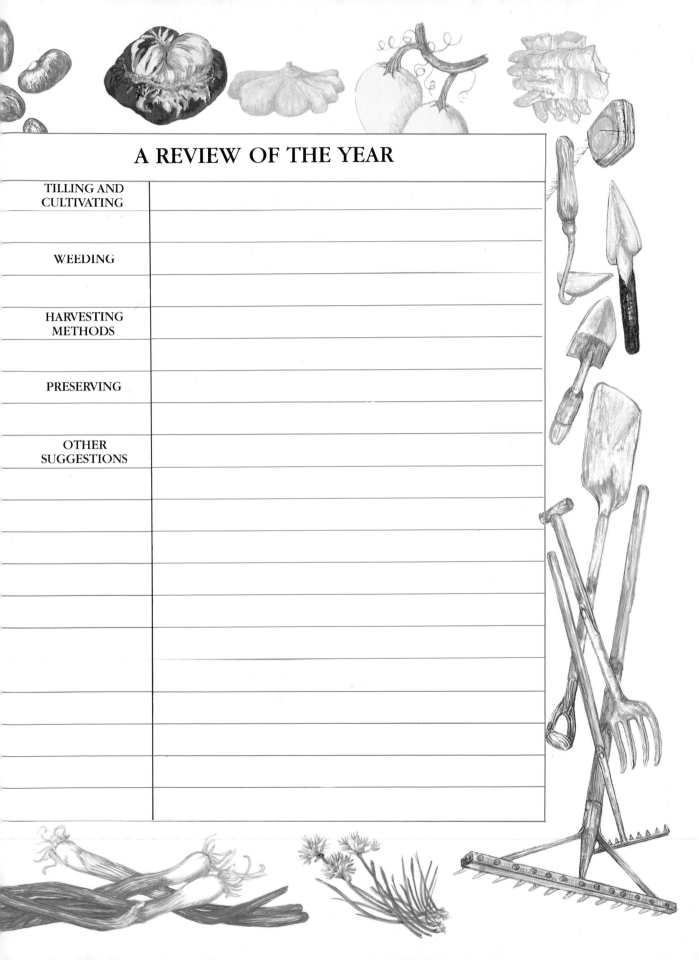

A REVIEW OF THE YEAR

TILLING AND CULTIVATING	
WEEDING	
HARVESTING METHODS	
PRESERVING	
OTHER SUGGESTIONS	

ACKNOWLEDGMENTS

The authors wish to thank W. Bradford Johnson, Extension Specialist in Vegetable Crops at Cook College, Rutgers University, for reading and commenting on the entire text; Stephanie and Dudley Head for their advice and suggestions throughout; Rosemary Foley for her critical role at the outset of the project; Roy Finamore for his skillful and perceptive editing; and Deborah Allen and Alfred Zalon for their understanding and patience as the book moved to completion.

Raphanus sativus

The text was set in ITC Garamond Book, and the display type in Folkwang, by U.S. Lithograph, Inc., New York, New York.

The book was printed and bound by Dai Nippon Printing Co., Ltd., Tokyo, Japan.